# Inspired Poems Volume 2
## Bisi Oladipupo

Springs of life publishing

Copyright © 2025  Bisi Oladipupo

Springs of life publishing

ISBN:   978-1-915269-49-2  (ePub e-book)

ISBN:   978-1-915269-48-5  (paperback)

All Rights Reserved.

No part of this book may be used or reproduced by any means, graphic, electronic, or mechanical, including photocopying, recording, taping, or by any information storage retrieval system without the written permission of the publisher except in the case of brief quotations embodied in critical articles and reviews.

Printed in the United Kingdom

# Contents

| | |
|---|---|
| Introduction | V |
| 1. Authority | 1 |
| 2. Be Bold | 3 |
| 3. Don't Be Weary | 5 |
| 4. Eternal Rewards | 6 |
| 5. Give God a Chance | 8 |
| 6. Give God something to work with | 10 |
| 7. He Wants to Move In | 11 |
| 8. He Wants to Move in (2) | 13 |
| 9. Hope Deferred | 14 |
| 10. Intimacy with God | 15 |
| 11. It is all about believing | 17 |

| | | |
|---|---|---|
| 12. | Joy | 19 |
| 13. | Prolonged Delay | 21 |
| 14. | Remove the Blinds | 23 |
| 15. | Strength | 25 |
| 16. | The Highway | 26 |
| | Gratitude | 27 |
| | Salvation Prayer | 28 |
| | About the author | 29 |
| | Also by | 30 |
| | Afterword | 32 |

# Introduction

This is my second book of poems, and I trust that they will bless you.

So, how did I start writing poems?

A fellow sister invited me to her event, where she presented poems at her local library. I decided to accept the invitation, so I went along.

Shortly after that, I found myself writing poems.

I believe I have tapped into a similar grace in her life, as she has written many poems.

Isn't the Lord so gracious?

You support others, and He blesses you.

I pray that these poems minister life to you.

# Authority

*Authority is not in volume,*
*But inside understanding lies the secret.*
*Jesus spoke with authority,*
*And the Master we must imitate,*

*The Son of Man drove out devils with a word,*
*And with a word did He cast out evil spirits.*
*Jesus used fewer words when He healed the sick,*
*And He said to him who was paralytic,*
*"Rise, take up your bed and walk."*

*Jesus used fewer words when He calmed the storm,*
*Unto it He said, "Peace be still", and the wind ceased.*
*When the Son of Man raised the dead,*
*He used fewer words:*

*"Young man, I say to you, arise," He said.*
*And the young man arose.*
*Jesus did not use many words,*
*As He is, so are we in this world;*
*We have been given authority*
*And with authority shall we speak.*

# Be Bold

*Boldness comes from the Lord*
*The Lord backs you up*
*That is why we can be bold*
*In the natural, if a great man backed you up*
*You will be bold*

*The Lord backs you up*
*His finished works back you up*
*The blood of Jesus speaks for you*
*Therefore be bold*

BISI OLADIPUPO

*The righteous are as bold as a lion*
*Because of Jesus*
*Be bold*
*Stand your ground and be bold*

# Don't Be Weary

*Your prayers avail much.*
*Doing much damage to the enemy's world.*
*I rise big in you,*
*I am in you,*
*My Spirit prays through you;*
*Victory is yours!*
*Victory is sure.*

# Eternal Rewards

*Our God is eternal*
*He lives forever*
*His Word is eternal*
*His covenant is eternal*
*We are eternal*
*His rewards are eternal*

*Whatever you do for the Lord*

## INSPIRED POEMS VOLUME 2

*Has eternal rewards*
*What a blessing*
*What a delight*
*Will you focus on eternal things in the temporary world?*

# Give God a Chance

*Did someone offend you?*
*Give God a chance.*
*Did someone betray you?*
*Give God a chance.*
*Did someone mislead you?*
*Give God a chance.*
*Did someone misrepresent Him to you?*
*Give God a chance*

*God is good*
*God is love*
*God is faithful*
*He loves you*
*Others may have failed*
*But give God a chance*
*They did not represent God*
*Forgive and move on in Him*
*Give to the One who loves you*
*A chance!*

# Give God something to work with

*The Lord needs your prayers for your needs*
*The Lord needs your words to produce life*
*The Lord needs your humility to promote you*
*The Lord needs your obedience to reward you*
*The Lord needs your patience to come through for you*
*Give God something to work with.*

# He Wants to Move In

*He wants to move in*
*Will you hear the knock*
*He wants to move in*
*With greater expression in you*
*Yes, you have said yes*
*But Jesus wants more of you*

*He wants full expression*

BISI OLADIPUPO

*So the world can see Him in you*
*Will you say yes to Jesus*
*I give you all of the room in my heart.*

# He Wants to Move in (2)

*He wants to move in*
*Will you open the door*
*He wants to move in*
*Will you respond to that knock*
*He wants to move in*
*Will you say yes*
*Jesus wants to move into your heart and life*

# Hope Deferred

*Hope may be deferred*
*But a tree of life is coming*
*When the desire is accomplished*
*Life flows*

*Delay does not mean denial*
*Hold unto hope*
*That hope will bring forth results*
*And you will see your heart rejoice*

# Intimacy with God

*Intimacy with God can be a lonely place;*
*Intimacy with God may not be popular;*
*But intimacy with God pays not just in this life,*
*Intimacy with God pays in the life to come,*
*For in it are eternal rewards.*

*Will you sacrifice that time off social media to be with God?*

*Will you put that phone off to be in God's presence?*
*The Lord says, "Come!"*
*Come closer;*
*Will you say yes?*

# It is all about believing

*Believing is the Kingdom's password*
*To come to the Lord, you must believe*
*To seek the Lord, you must believe*
*To get an answer to prayer, you must believe*
*To have what you say, you must believe*

*Believing is the first thing in God's kingdom*
*All things are possible to him who believes*

BISI OLADIPUPO

*Invest in your belief system*
*And begin to see God at work*

# Joy

The joy of the Lord cannot be contained
O, the unspeakable joy of the Lord!
Where does that joy come from?
From our union with Christ.
Let nothing take that joy from you
Jesus is the source of your joy

Joy beyond words,
Joy without measure,
Yes, the unspeakable joy of the Lord

BISI OLADIPUPO

Full of glory!

# Prolonged Delay

*Prolonged delay is not denial*
*Sometimes things are delayed*
*And we know not why*
*Unto Abraham a child was promised*
*But it took 25 years to have Isaac*
*Isaac was also delayed*
*And it took 20 years to have Jacob and Esau*

*In it all*
*God won*
*Abraham was blessed*
*All the nations of the earth are blessed*
*Because of Abraham*
*They looked delayed, but it came to pass*
*Has the Lord promised you something?*

*Do you have a vision from the Lord?*
*It may look delayed*
*Hang on there*
*Stay in the process*
*They are still steps*
*And see that delay manifest*
*Into what God has said*

# Remove the Blinds

*The blinds off your loved ones*
*The blinds off your friends*
*The enemy places blinds on people's minds*
*Wrong perceptions about God*
*Wrong perceptions about what this walk is all about*
*They are barriers hindering the glorious gospel*
*So that it will not shine upon them*
*So get on your knees*

*Intercede*
*Remove the blinds in prayer*
*And see many flock to the Lord*
*They will see*
*And respond to the glorious gospel of Christ.*

# Strength

*Be strong in the Lord*
*And in the power of His might*
*You can do all things*
*Through Christ who strengthens you*
*The Lord Almighty*
*Mighty in strength*
*He is the One who strengthens you*
*Your strength is in Him*
*So be strong in Him*

# The Highway

*The highway is walking in the Spirit*
*The highway is saying yes to God*
*The highway is laying down our own agenda*
*The highway is walking in partnership with the Holy Spirit*
*That is the highway*
*That is the way for those in Christ*
*Stay on the highway*
*Don't yield to the flesh*
*And you will reap many benefits in Him.*

# Gratitude

Firstly, I want to acknowledge my Lord and Saviour Jesus Christ, the giver of gifts.

I also want to thank God for leading me to support a friend, Sophia, when she had a poetry day at her local library a few years ago.

After that event, I found that I started writing poetry.

What an awesome God we serve. You support others, and He blesses you.

# Salvation Prayer

Father God, I come to you in Jesus' name. I admit that I am a sinner, and I now receive the sacrifice that Jesus Christ paid for me.

I confess with my mouth the Lord Jesus, and I believe in my heart that God raised Him from the dead.

I now declare that Jesus Christ is my Lord and Saviour.

Thank you, Father, for saving me in Jesus' name.

I am now your child. Amen.

If you've said this prayer for the first time, please send an email to Bisiwriter@gmail.com.

Start reading your Bible and ask the Lord to guide you to a good church. Additionally, ask the Lord for good Christian friends who will support and help you along this new journey.

# About the author

For many years, Bisi Oladipupo has been a Christian and lives in the UK with her family. She's a graduate of multiple Bible colleges, including a UK leadership program. Additionally, she graduated from a U.S. ministry school with a Bachelor's degree in Bible and Theology. Bisi teaches God's Word and leads Bible studies and Christian fellowship groups. Visit her website and author page located at www.bisiwrites.com and www.bisiwrites.org.

Bisi can be reached at bisiwriter@gmail.com for enquiries.

# Also by

1. The Twelve Apostles of Jesus Christ: Lessons We Can Learn
2. The Lord's Cup in Communion: The Significance of taking the Lord's Supper
3. Different Ways to Receive Healing from Scripture and Walk in Health
4. Believing on The Name of Jesus Christ: What Every Believer Needs to Know
5. The Mind and Your Christian Walk: The Impact of the mind on our Christian walk
6. Relationship Skills in the Bible: Scriptural Principles of relating to others
7. The Nature of God's Kingdom: The Characteristics of the Kingdom of God
8. The Person of the Holy Spirit

9. 41 Insights from the Book of Revelation
10. The Importance of Spiritual Discernment
11. God Speaks Through Nature
12. It's All About the Heart
13. A Better Covenant: A Look at the Covenants of God and Our Better Covenant
14. 40 Day New Covenant Devotional
15. What Happens When We Pray ?
16. Daily Bread for Healing: A 40-day Healing Devotional
17. 40 Facts of Who Jesus Is: A Devotional
18. 50 Prayers for Your Children and Generations to Come
19. The Grace of God: Why We Need It
20. The Importance of Spiritual Understanding
21. In Christ: Who We Are and What We Have in Him : 40 Daily Bites
22. Inspired Poems Volume 1

# Afterword

If you enjoyed this book, please take a few moments to write a review of it online at the store where it was purchased. Thank you.

www.ingramcontent.com/pod-product-compliance
Lightning Source LLC
Chambersburg PA
CBHW060344080526
44584CB00013B/918